SAUDI ARABIA 2012 HUMAN RIGHTS REPORT

EXECUTIVE SUMMARY

The Kingdom of Saudi Arabia is a monarchy ruled by King Abdullah bin Abdulaziz Al Saud, who is both head of state and head of government. The government bases its legitimacy on its interpretation of Sharia (Islamic law) and the 1992 Basic Law, which specifies that the rulers of the country shall be male descendants of the founder King Abdulaziz bin Abdulrahman Al Saud. The Basic Law sets out the system of governance, rights of citizens, and powers and duties of the government, and it provides that the Quran and Sunna (the traditions of the Prophet Muhammad) serve as the country's constitution. In September 2011 the country held elections on a nonparty basis for half of the 1,632 seats on the 285 municipal councils around the country. Independent polling station observers identified no irregularities with the election; however, women were not candidates and did not vote. Security forces reported to civilian authorities.

The most important human rights problems reported included citizens' lack of the right and legal means to change their government; pervasive restrictions on universal rights such as freedom of expression, including on the Internet, and freedom of assembly, association, movement, and religion; and a lack of equal rights for women, children, and expatriate workers.

Other human rights problems reported included torture and other abuses; overcrowding in prisons and detention centers; holding political prisoners and detainees; denial of due process; arbitrary arrest and detention; and arbitrary interference with privacy, home, and correspondence. Violence against women, trafficking in persons, and discrimination based on gender, religion, sect, race, and ethnicity were common. Lack of governmental transparency and access made it difficult to assess the magnitude of many reported human rights problems.

The government identified, prosecuted, and punished a limited number of officials who committed abuses, particularly those engaged in or complicit with corruption. Some members of the security forces and other senior officials, including those linked to the royal family, reportedly committed abuses with relative impunity.

Section 1.Respect for the Integrity of the Person, Including Freedom from:

a. Arbitrary or Unlawful Deprivation of Life

The government or its agents were not known to have committed politically motivated killings during the year. Closed court proceedings in capital cases made it impossible to determine positively whether the accused were allowed to present a defense or were granted basic due process; however, in November the Law on Criminal Procedure was amended to require a unanimous endorsement by the Supreme Judicial Council for all death sentences.

There were reports that security forces killed persons during clashes with demonstrators, who were sometimes armed.

On July 9, protesters demonstrated following the arrest and wounding of Shia cleric Sheikh Nimr al-Nimr. Two people were killed in subsequent protests. YouTube videos showed one protest with a crowd walking down a street when gunshots became audible. The videos showed several of the injured, including one covered in blood, being carried away. At year's end there were no reports of any action taken because of the killing of the demonstrators.

During separate conflicts with police during protests on February 9 and 10, Munir al-Mudani was killed in downtown Qatif as well as Zahir al-Saeed in Awamiya, according to local media reports. International media reported as many as 50 people were injured during the two incidents. Additionally, on January 12, Essam al-Abdullah died following police raids in Awamiya. Demonstrators were calling for an end to sectarian discrimination and the release of Shia detainees. The government claimed that youths attacked security forces with Molotov cocktails and that an "exchange of fire" between protesters and security forces resulted in the death and injuries; however, protesters' accounts of the incident contended that security forces responded to stone-throwing youths by firing indiscriminately at protestors.

According to the country's practice of Sharia, capital punishment is the prescribed penalty for sorcery. Sorcery is distinguished from the practice of magic or witchcraft in that it necessarily involves an act or intent to inflict physical or psychological harm on another person. The country lacks a written penal code listing criminal offenses and the associated penalties for them (see section 1. e.); absent such a code, the punishments for the practice of magic or sorcery are subject to considerable judicial discretion in the courts.

On June 19, officials beheaded Muree bin Ali al-Asiri in the southern province of Najran for "practicing witchcraft and sorcery" and "for owning written talismans."

According to press reports, officials executed bin Ali al-Asiri after the Supreme Judicial Council upheld his sentence.

b. Disappearance

The government reportedly arrested and detained persons during the year, refusing for extended periods in some cases to acknowledge the detention or to provide information about an individual's whereabouts. However, there were no reports of politically motivated disappearances during the year.

c. Torture and Other Cruel, Inhuman, or Degrading Treatment or Punishment

The law prohibits torture and holds criminal investigation officers accountable for any abuse of authority. Sharia, as interpreted in the country, prohibits judges from accepting confessions obtained under duress; statutory law provides that public investigators shall not subject accused persons to coercive measures to influence their testimony.

Government officials claimed that Ministry of Interior (MOI) rules prohibiting torture prevented such practices from occurring in the penal system. They also claimed representatives from the governmental Human Rights Commission (HRC) and the quasi-nongovernmental National Society for Human Rights (NSHR), which is supported by a trust funded by the estate of the late King Fahd, conducted prison visits to ascertain that torture did not occur in prisons or detention centers. Nevertheless, during the year there continued to be reports that authorities sometimes subjected prisoners and detainees to torture and other physical abuse, particularly during the investigation phase when interrogating suspects; however, due to lack of government transparency, it was not possible to ascertain the accuracy of these reports. There was no available information on the number of cases of abuse and corporal punishment.

For example, in July 2011 security officials reportedly took human rights activist Mekhlef bin Daham al-Shammary from his prison cell at the Damman General Prison and allegedly poured an antiseptic cleaning liquid down his throat, resulting in his being taken to a hospital. Officials released al-Shammary from prison on March 8. Also during the year, the Board of Grievances reportedly awarded al-Shammary compensation for wrongful detention (see section 1.e.).

In an unrelated case, the father of Khalid bin Fahad al-Shammary submitted a complaint in October to the Riyadh administrative court claiming his son died from torture and mistreatment by officers from the MOI's General Investigation Directorate (Mabahith, the internal security police) following his arrest in Hail Province in 2006. According to the complaint, investigators beat al-Shammary with chairs, hung him for several days in his cell, and restrained him with handcuffs and leg cuffs for 28 days in Turfiyya Prison in Hail. The complaint named Mabahith officer Abdul Aziz al-Ahmadi as one of the perpetrators of the abuse and claimed al-Shammary died in the Security Forces Hospital, Riyadh, after a massive deterioration in his medical condition resulting from the alleged abuse and denial of medical care. At year's end there was no action on the complaint.

Additionally, 16 men found guilty of security-related offenses in December 2011 and sentenced to prison terms ranging from five to 30 years remained in prison at year's end (see section 3.)

The Commission for the Promotion of Virtue and Prevention of Vice (CPVPV), a semiautonomous agency commonly known as the religious police, has authority to monitor social behavior and enforce morality subject to the law and in coordination with law enforcement authorities (see section 1.d.).

During the year several CPVPV members in Medina who assaulted a woman were convicted in Medina administrative court for abuse of power. The conviction followed a two-month investigation by the Control and Investigation Board. CPVPV members believed that the woman and her uncle were not related and engaged in immoral gender mixing; they assaulted the woman and her uncle while the two were taking a taxi through the city. When the CPVPV members recognized their error, they attempted to bribe the woman and her uncle in exchange for their silence; however, the woman submitted a formal complaint to the governor of Medina, who initiated the investigation that resulted in the CPVPV members' suspension.

The courts continued to use corporal punishment as a judicial penalty, including floggings and amputation, as well as public execution by beheading. On November 21, Mohammed Ahmed Ibrahim had his right hand amputated in Mecca after being found guilty of theft; according to an official announcement, the Court of Appeals and the Supreme Court upheld the punishment.

Prison and Detention Center Conditions

Prison and detention center conditions varied, and some did not meet international standards.

Physical Conditions: The director general of prisons announced in October 2011 that there were 49,000 male and female prisoners and detainees in the kingdom. Although information on the maximum capacity of the facilities was not available, overcrowding in prisons and detention centers was a problem. In February 2011, after visiting 16 jails across the kingdom, the NSHR reported that "most jails are operating at double their capacities, something that denies inmates many of their basic rights." The report also noted a number of other problems in prisons and detention centers, the worst being the women's section of the Deportation and Detention Center in Jeddah. Violations listed in the report included a shortage of and improperly trained wardens, lack of access to prompt medical treatment when requested, holding prisoners beyond the end of their sentences, and not informing prisoners of their legal rights.

Pretrial detainees were held together with convicted prisoners. Persons suspected or convicted of terrorism offenses were separated from the general population but held in similar facilities. There were no reports of prisoners being denied access to potable water.

Administration: Recordkeeping on prisoners was inadequate. There were several reports that prisoners were held after their sentences were completed. No ombudsmen were available to register or investigate complaints made by prisoners, although prisoners could and did submit complaints to the HRC and the NSHR for investigation. Authorities differentiated between violent and nonviolent prisoners, pardoning nonviolent prisoners to reduce the prison population.

Relatives and friends were permitted to visit prisoners twice per week; however, there were reports of this privilege being denied by prison officials in some instances. Muslim detainees and prisoners were permitted to perform religious observances. There was no information available whether prisoners were able to submit complaints to judicial authorities without censorship or whether credible allegations of inhumane conditions and treatment were investigated and made public.

Monitoring: No independent human rights observers visited prisons or detention centers during the year, but the government permitted the governmental HRC and domestic organizations such as the NSHR to monitor prison conditions. The organizations reported that they visited prisons throughout the country and reported on prison conditions. The NSHR monitored health care in prisons and brought deficiencies to the attention of the MOI, which administers prisons and detention centers. In its annual report, the NSHR registered 759 cases in 2011 involving prisoners and detainees who complained about conditions, compared with 709 cases in 2010.

d. Arbitrary Arrest or Detention

The law provides that no entity may restrict a person's actions or imprison him, except under provisions of the law. A person under arrest may not be detained legally for more than 24 hours, except pursuant to a written order from a public investigator. Authorities must inform the detained person of the reasons for detention. Nonetheless, because of the government's ambiguous implementation of the law and a lack of due process, the MOI, to which the majority of forces with arrest power report, maintained broad powers to arrest and detain persons indefinitely without judicial oversight or effective access to legal counsel or family. In practice authorities held persons for weeks, months, and sometimes years and reportedly failed to advise them promptly of their rights, including their legal right to be represented by an attorney.

Role of the Police and Security Apparatus

The king, interior minister, defense minister, and national guard commander all have responsibility in law and in practice for law enforcement and maintenance of order. The MOI exercised primary control over internal security and police forces. The civil police and the internal security police are authorized to arrest and detain individuals. The semiautonomous CPVPV, which monitors public behavior to enforce strict adherence to the official interpretation of Islamic norms, reports to the king via the Royal Diwan (royal court) and to the MOI. The members of the religious police are required to carry official identification and have a police officer accompany them at the time of an arrest. The head of the CPVPV, Sheikh Abdullatif Al al-Sheikh (appointed in January), ordered strict compliance with this policy and prohibited any nonofficial volunteers. In an October 15 public address to youth, he emphasized citizens need not listen to any professed CPVPV member not displaying official identification. In addition Al al-Sheikh reiterated in a meeting with CPVPV branch directors that CPVPV officials are not allowed to pursue individuals but rather are to take note of relevant information and refer it to the police for further action, including arrest.

Security forces were generally effective at maintaining law and order. The Board of Grievances (Diwan al-Mazalim), a high-level administrative judicial body that specializes in cases against government entities and reports directly to the king, is the only formal mechanism available to seek redress for claims of abuse. Citizens may report abuses by security forces at any police station, to the HRC, or to the NSHR. The HRC and the NSHR maintained records of complaints and outcomes, but privacy laws protected information about individual cases, and information was not publicly available. During the year there were no reported prosecutions of security forces for human rights violations, but the Board of Grievances held hearings and adjudicated claims of wrongdoing. The HRC, in cooperation with the Ministry of Education, provided materials and training to police, security forces, and the religious police on protecting human rights.

The Bureau of Investigation and Prosecution (BIP) and the Control and Investigation Board (CIB) are the two units of the government with authority to investigate reports of criminal activity, corruption, and "disciplinary cases" involving government employees. These bodies are responsible for investigating potential cases and referring them to the administrative courts.

In November 2011 the Council of Ministers consolidated legal authorities for investigation and public prosecution of criminal offences within the BIP; however, the CIB continued to be responsible for investigation and prosecution of noncriminal cases. All financial audit and control functions were limited to the General Auditing Board.

Arrest Procedures and Treatment While in Detention

According to the Law of Criminal Procedure, "no person shall be arrested, searched, detained, or imprisoned except in cases provided by law, and any accused person shall have the right to seek the assistance of a lawyer or a representative to defend him during the investigation and trial stages." Authorities may summon any person for investigation, and an arrest warrant may be issued based on evidence, but in practice warrants frequently were not used, and they were not required in cases where probable cause existed.

The law requires charges be filed within 72 hours of arrest and requires a trial within six months. Legally, a person under arrest may not be detained for more than 24 hours, except pursuant to a written order from a public investigator. Authorities reportedly often failed to observe these legal protections, and there was no requirement to advise suspects of their rights. In practice no judicial proceedings began until a full investigation was completed by authorities, which in some cases took years.

There was a functioning bail system for less serious criminal charges. The law does not specify a time frame for access to a lawyer. The practice is for the state to provide a lawyer for indigents.

The international nongovernmental organization Amnesty International (AI) reported in a September 5 bulletin that Khaled al-Johani was released on August 8 after having been arrested in Riyadh in March 2011. Authorities reportedly detained al-Johani, a 40-year-old teacher, after he conducted an interview with BBC Arabic where he criticized the lack of freedom in the country. According to the AI bulletin, between his initial detention and February 22 trial before the Specialized Criminal Court, authorities placed al-Johani in solitary confinement for at least two months, did not allow him to choose a lawyer, and did not inform him of the charges against him.

Incommunicado detention was sometimes a problem. There were no established procedures providing detainees the right to contact family members following arrest. Frequently security and some other prisoners remained in detention for long periods before family members or associates received information of their whereabouts.

Arbitrary Arrest: There were reports of arbitrary arrest and detention. Although the law prohibits detention without charge for periods longer than six months, during the year authorities detained without charge security suspects, persons who publicly criticized the government, Shia religious leaders, and persons who violated religious standards.

Pretrial Detention: Lengthy pretrial detention was a problem. The nongovernmental organization (NGO) Saudi Civil and Political Rights Association (ACPRA) challenged the MOI publicly and in court on cases considered to involve arbitrary arrest or detention; however, the ACPRA claimed the ministry ignored judges' rulings, and judges appeared powerless to take action against the ministry. There was no available information on the percentage of the prison detainee population in pretrial detention or the average length of time held. Human rights activists reportedly received eight to 10 calls per week from families claiming their relatives were being held arbitrarily.

On December 10, *Time World* published a report on Ghazi al-Harbi, a military officer at King Faisal Air Base in Tabuk, who reportedly was arrested in 2005 and accused of "conspiring to commit treason" and "proposing demonstrations against the state." Al-Harbi reported he spent four years in jail before he had the opportunity to defend himself against the charges. A judge sentenced him to time served and ordered him released; however, the MOI overruled the judge's decision and kept al-Harbi in prison for three additional years, until they released him in February.

On April 2, the MOI's Bureau of Investigation and Prosecution released statistics accounting for those detained for suspicion of terrorism since 2001. The data suggested that roughly half of the 11,527 persons arrested had been released. Of those not released, 2,215 had been referred to "the competent criminal courts," with 1,612 convicted by April 2; the others were still being tried. There were 1,931 detainees nearing transfer to court as investigations were being completed, 934 detainees were still being held pending final charges, and another 616 were "still pending trial," although it was not clear what that description meant. The MOI also reportedly paid compensation of 32 million riyals ($8.5 million) to 486 detainees for being held longer in detention than their jail sentences and provided 529 million riyals ($141 million) in monthly assistance to the families of suspects.

Amnesty: The king continued the tradition of commuting some judicial punishments. The details of the cases varied, but the demonstration of royal pardons sometimes included reducing or eliminating corporal punishment, for example, rather than set aside the conviction. However, the remaining sentence could be added to a new sentence if the pardoned prisoner committed a crime subsequent to his release. There were pardons or grants of amnesty on special occasions throughout the year. The Saudi Press Agency reported that at least 1,543 prisoners were pardoned and released during the year. In addition the agency reported 325 of 1,719 Indonesian prisoners were pardoned during the year.

e. Denial of Fair Public Trial

The law provides that judges are independent and are subject to no authority other than the provisions of Sharia and laws in force. In practice the judiciary was not independent, as it was required to coordinate its decisions with executive authorities with the king as final arbiter. Although allegations of interference with judicial independence were rare, the judiciary was reportedly subject to influence. There were no reports during the year of courts exercising jurisdiction over senior members of the royal family, and it is not clear whether the judiciary would have jurisdiction in such instances. There were problems allegedly enforcing court orders, particularly against the MOI.

Trial Procedures

The law states that defendants should be treated equally in accordance with Sharia. In the absence of a written penal code listing criminal offenses and punishments, these penalties are determined by legal interpretations of Sharia by judges in the courts. The Council of Senior Religious Scholars, an autonomous advisory body, issues religious opinions (fatwas) that guide how judges interpret Sharia.

Additionally, Sharia is not solely based on precedent. As a result, rulings and sentences can diverge widely from case to case. Judges may base their decisions on any of the four Sunni schools of jurisprudence; however, in practice the Hanbali School is predominant and forms the basis for the country's law and legal interpretations of Sharia. Shia citizens use their legal traditions to adjudicate family law cases between Shia parties; however, either party can decide to adjudicate a case in state courts, which use Sunni legal tradition.

According to the law, there is neither presumption of innocence nor trial by jury. The law requires a person cannot be held more than 24 hours without a written order from a BIP investigator who must obtain a statement from the accused regarding innocence or guilt of the specific charge and determine whether there is sufficient evidence to hold the person longer. The law states that court hearings shall be public; however, courts may be closed at the judge's discretion, and as a result many trials during the year were closed. According to the Ministry of Justice, a trial may be closed depending on the sensitivity of the case to national security, the reputation of the defendant, or the safety of witnesses. During the year the government continued to try suspected terrorists. These trials nominally were open to observers from the HRC, the media, and the public; however, observers required advance approval from the MOI.

According to the HRC at the government's discretion, an attorney may be provided to indigents at public expense. The law provides defendants the right to be present at trial and to consult with an attorney during the investigation and trial. There is no right to access government-held evidence. Defendants may request to review evidence, and the court decides whether to grant the request. Defendants also have the right to confront or question witnesses against them and call witnesses on their behalf. However, the court presents the witnesses. The law provides that an investigator appointed by the BIP questions the witnesses called by the litigants before the initiation of a trial and may hear testimony of additional witnesses he deems necessary to determine the facts. A defendant may not be compelled to take an oath or subjected to any coercive measures. The court must inform convicted persons of their right to appeal rulings.

Sharia, as interpreted by the government, extends these provisions to all citizens and noncitizens; however, the law and practice discriminate against women (see section 6), nonpracticing Sunni, Shia, foreigners, and persons of other religions. For example, judges may discount the testimony of nonpracticing Sunni Muslims, Shia Muslims, or persons of other religions; sources reported that judges sometimes completely ignored testimony by Shia.

Among many reports of irregularities in trial procedures was the case of Mohammed Saleh al-Bajady, a cofounder of the ACPRA, whom police arrested in March 2011 in Buraidah, Qassim Province, a day after his participation in a protest outside the MOI in Riyadh. On April 10, the Specialized Criminal Court found Bajady guilty of unlawfully establishing an unlicensed human rights NGO and sentenced him to four years in prison to be followed by a five-year travel ban. During Bajady's trial the court denied observers access to hearings and refused to acknowledge his lawyer.

In August 2011 the Royal Diwan forwarded the case of Rizana Nafeek to the Riyadh Provincial Reconciliation Committee to negotiate a settlement between Nafeek, a Sri Lankan domestic worker, and the parents of an infant she was convicted of having killed. At year's end the infant's family had refused to pardon the maid or accept compensation and demanded that authorities carry out Nafeek's death sentence.

Political Prisoners and Detainees

The number of political prisoners or detainees who reportedly remained in prolonged detention without charge could not be reliably ascertained. In a report MOI spokesperson General Mansour al-Turki noted that of the 11,000 people officially arrested on security-related charges, 50 percent were in prison. However, on December 9, local media reported there were 2,709 detainees, including 597 foreign nationals, facing security-related charges in five prisons. In many cases it was impossible to determine the legal basis for incarceration and whether the detention complied with international norms and standards. Those who remained imprisoned after trial often were convicted of terrorism-related crimes, and there was not sufficient public information about such alleged crimes to judge whether they had a credible claim to be political prisoners.

International NGOs, AI in particular, criticized the government for abusing its antiterrorism prerogatives to arrest some members of the political opposition. Security detainees were generally given the same protections as other prisoners or detainees. High-profile prisoners generally were well treated. Certain prisoners, held on terrorism-related charges, were given the option to participate in government-sponsored rehabilitation programs. Authorities sometimes restricted legal access to detainees (see section 1.d.); no international humanitarian organizations had access to them.

On December 15, a court sentenced Shia cleric Tawfiq al-Amer to three years in prison followed by a five-year travel ban. Detained in August 2011 for comments critical of the government, al-Amer was charged in November with, among other offenses, calling for political change, libeling the country's religious scholars, and collecting illegal religious donations.

On July 8, security forces arrested Shia cleric Nimr al-Nimr, who sustained a gunshot wound to his left leg in the process; no charges were known to have been filed against him. Following his arrest Nimr went on a 45-day hunger strike; after medical treatment and a hospital stay, he was transferred to Ha'ir prison outside Riyadh, where he remained at year's end. Family members were allowed to visit al-Nimr.

Civil Judicial Procedures and Remedies

Complainants claiming human rights violations generally sought assistance from the HRC or NSHR, which either advocated on their behalf or provided courts with opinions on their cases. The HRC was generally responsive to complaints; domestic violence cases were the most common. However, individuals or organizations may also directly petition for damages or government action to end human rights violations before the Board of Grievances.

Human rights activist Mekhlef bin Daham al-Shammary (see section 1.c.) filed a complaint against the government and demanded compensation for unnecessary suffering because of being imprisoned for more than four months in 2007. Al-Shammary was arrested for repeatedly holding unauthorized political meetings. On November 25, the Board of Grievances ordered the Bureau of Investigation and

Prosecution to pay al-Shammary 190,000 riyals ($50,667) for wrongful detention between 2008 and 2009.

In 2010 the MOI's General Investigation Directorate (Mabahith) arrested human rights activist and student Thamer Abdulkareem al-Kather without charge in Qassim and transferred him to a prison in Riyadh. Al-Kather had advocated for prisoners' rights and constitutional reform. In June 2011 the Board of Grievances ruled that al-Kather was being held arbitrarily and should be released, but the MOI appealed the verdict. In February al-Kather was released without charge.

In August 2011 the Board of Grievances ordered Jeddah police to pay 152,700 riyals ($40,720) to a man detained for almost three years without trial. The police reportedly had forgotten about him and his case.

f. Arbitrary Interference with Privacy, Family, Home, or Correspondence

The law prohibits unlawful intrusions into the privacy of persons, their homes, places of work, and vehicles. Criminal investigation officers are required to maintain records of all searches conducted; these records should contain the name of the officer conducting the search, the text of the search warrant (or an explanation of the urgency that necessitated the search without a warrant), and the names and signatures of the persons who were present at the time of search. While the law also provides for the privacy of all mail, cables, telephone conversations, and other means of communication, the government did not respect the privacy of correspondence or communications, and the government used the considerable latitude provided by the law to monitor activities legally and intervene where it deemed necessary.

There were reports from human rights activists of governmental monitoring or blocking mobile telephone or Internet usage before planned demonstrations. The government strictly monitored politically related activities and took punitive actions, including arrest and detention, against persons who engaged in certain political activities, such as direct public criticism of some senior royals by name, forming a political party, or organizing a demonstration. Customs officials reportedly routinely opened mail and shipments to search for contraband. In some areas MOI informants allegedly reported "seditious ideas," "antigovernment activity," or "behavior contrary to Islam" in their neighborhoods.

The CPVPV monitored and regulated public interaction between members of the opposite sex.

Section 2. Respect for Civil Liberties, Including:

a. Freedom of Speech and Press

The government charged a number of individuals with crimes related to their exercise of free speech during the year. Specifically, the government charged those using the Internet to express dissent with subversion, blasphemy, and apostasy.

Government-friendly ownership in print or broadcast media led to self-censorship, and there was relatively little need for overt government action to restrict freedom of expression. However, the government could not rely on self-censoring in social media and the Internet. Accordingly, to control information, it monitored and blocked certain Internet sites. On a number of occasions, government officials and senior clerics publicly warned against inaccurate reports on the Internet and reminded the public that criticism of the government and its officials should be done through available private channels.

Freedom of Speech: The government monitored public expressions of opinion and took advantage of legal controls to impede the free expression of opinion and restrict those verging on the political sphere. Public employees are prohibited from directly or indirectly engaging in dialogue with local or foreign media or participating in any meetings intended to oppose state policies. The law forbids apostasy and blasphemy, which can carry the death penalty.

On December 24, writer Turki al-Hamad reportedly was arrested after publishing Twitter comments critical of Islamists and political Islam; at year's end he remained in detention without charge, but his family was allowed to visit him. The Riyadh-based NGO Global Commission for Introducing the Messenger claimed it requested the interior minister detain al-Hamad for his controversial comments.

On February 12, blogger Hamza Kashgari was arrested in Malaysia and returned to the country on charges of blasphemy after publishing a poem February 4 on Twitter deemed insulting to the Prophet Mohammed. Upon his return Kashgari issued a full apology and "repented." A Riyadh court reportedly accepted Kashgari's repentance, and he was transferred to Dhahban Prison in Jeddah in order to be closer to his family. He remained in detention at year's end.

On December 17, a court in Jeddah referred the case of Ra'if Badawi to a higher court on charges of apostasy. A human rights activist and the founder of the Saudi Liberal Network on the Internet, an online social forum, Badawi was detained in June after his father charged him with "disobedience" in connection with the online forum. He was charged with responsibility for the comments posted on this Web site, which were characterized as violating Islamic values, encouraging blasphemy and mocking Islamic religious symbols. According to media sources, Badawi was also charged with violating Islamic values and mocking Islamic religious symbols on his Web site.

In March 2011 Internet activists urged people to demonstrate in favor of political and economic reforms. Despite warnings from religious and government leaders and a strong security presence, one teacher, Khaled al-Johani, did so. Police arrested al-Johani immediately after he spoke to media about the need to "speak freely" and have "freedom" and "democracy. He was released on August 8, and there was no record he was charged with an offense (see section 1.d.).

In June a Jeddah court charged human rights lawyer and activist Waleed Abu al-Khair with "tarnishing" the image of the kingdom and contempt of the judiciary. Abu al-Khair, who also supervises the Facebook group Saudi Human Rights Monitor, was also charged in September 2011 for criticizing the government. Authorities summoned him to court in Jeddah on multiple occasions, but at year's end he had not been tried but was restricted from travel outside the country.

Freedom of Press: The Press and Publications Law, extending explicitly to Internet communications, governs printed materials; printing presses; bookstores; import, rent, and sale of films; television and radio; and foreign media offices and their correspondents. In April 2011 a royal decree amended the law to strengthen penalties and created a special commission to judge violations. The decree banned publishing anything "contradicting Sharia; inciting disruption; serving foreign interests that contradict national interests; and damaging the reputation of the Grand Mufti, members of the Council of Senior Religious Scholars, or senior government officials." The Ministry of Culture and Information may permanently close "whenever necessary" any means of communication--defined as any means of expressing any viewpoint that is meant for circulation--that it deems is engaged in a prohibited activity as set forth in the April 2011 royal decree. Print and broadcast media, already self-censored, did not appear to have been demonstrably affected by these restrictions.

The government owned most print and broadcast media and book publication facilities in the country, and members of the royal family owned or influenced those that were privately owned and nominally independent, including various media outlets and widely circulated pan-Arab newspapers such as *Ash-Sharq Al-Awsat* and *Al-Hayat*. The government owned, operated, and censored most domestic television and radio outlets.

Satellite television dish usage was widespread. Although satellite dishes technically were illegal, the government did not enforce restrictions on satellite dishes. Access to foreign sources of information, including the Internet, was common. Privately owned satellite television networks headquartered outside the country maintained local offices and operated under a system of self-censorship. Many foreign satellite stations broadcast a wide range of programs into the country, in English and Arabic, including foreign news channels such as CNN, Fox, BBC, Sky, and al-Jazeera. Foreign media are subject to licensing requirements from the Ministry of Culture and Information and cannot operate freely.

The Ministry of Culture and Information must approve appointment of all senior editors and has authority to remove them. The government provides guidelines to newspapers regarding controversial issues. A 1982 media policy statement urges journalists to uphold Islam, oppose atheism, promote Arab interests, and preserve cultural heritage. The Saudi Press Agency reports official government news.

All newspapers in the country must be government-licensed. Media outlets can legally be banned or have their publication temporarily halted if the government concludes they violated the Press and Publications Law.

Censorship or Content Restrictions: The government reportedly penalized those who published items counter to government guidelines and directly or indirectly censored the media by licensing domestic media and by controlling importation of foreign printed material. Authorities prevented or delayed the distribution of foreign print media, effectively censoring these publications. However, in some cases individuals criticized specific government bodies or actions publicly without repercussions.

In September 2011 Fahad al-Aqran, the editor in chief of *Al-Madina*, and Abdulaziz al-Sowaid, a columnist for *Al-Madina*, were fired and referred to the Ministry of Culture and Information's review board after the columnist wrote an article with controversial interpretations of theological issues. At year's end there was no further information available.

The Consultative Council (Majlis as-Shura), an advisory body, frequently allowed print and broadcast media to observe its proceedings and meetings, but the council closed some high-profile or controversial sessions to the media. For example, on May 28, media reported that the council sat in closed session with the minister of labor to discuss introduction of a minimum wage and other labor issues.

Internet Freedom

The Press and Publications Law already implicitly covered the electronic media, since it extended to any means of expression of a viewpoint meant for circulation, ranging from words to cartoons, photographs, and sounds. In March 2011 the government issued "Implementing Regulations of Electronic Publishing," setting out rules for Internet-based and other electronic media, including chat rooms, personal blogs, and text messages.

The Press and Publications Law criminalizes the publication or downloading of offensive sites. The governmental Communications and Information Technology Commission (CITC) filtered and blocked access to Web sites it deemed offensive including some pages calling for political, social, or economic reforms or human rights; there were credible reports that it monitored e-mail and Internet chat rooms. Under security regulations Internet cafe owners were required to install cameras and keep records on their users. The law restricted the ability of individuals and groups to engage in the expression of views via the Internet, including by e-mail.

The Ministry of Culture and Information or its agencies must authorize all Web sites registered and hosted in the country. The CITC dealt with requests to block adult content and coordinated decisions with the Saudi Arabian Monetary Agency on blocking phishing sites seeking to obtain confidential personal or financial information. Under the Telecommunication Act, failure by service providers to block banned sites can result in a fine of five million riyals ($1.33 million). All other requests to block sites were submitted to an interagency committee, chaired by the MOI, for a decision to block a site or not. In addition to designating unacceptable sites, the CITC accepted requests from citizens to block or unblock sites. According to the CITC, authorities received an average of 200 requests daily to block and unblock sites. According to the NGO Reporters Without Borders, authorities claimed to have blocked approximately 400,000 Web sites. CITC claimed Facebook removed materials the CITC deemed offensive, but Twitter ignored all CITC requests.

Access to the Internet was legally available only through government-authorized Internet service providers. Although the authorities blocked Web sites offering proxies, persistent Internet users could work around the blocked sites and continue to access the Internet via other proxy servers.

Laws criminalize defamation on the Internet, hacking, unauthorized access to government Web sites, and stealing information related to national security, as well as the creation or dissemination of a Web site for a terrorist organization. The government reportedly collected personally identifiable information concerning the identity of persons peacefully expressing political, religious, or ideological opinions or beliefs.

Academic Freedom and Cultural Events

The government censored public artistic expression, prohibited cinemas, and restricted public musical or theatrical performances apart from those considered folkloric and special events approved by the government. Academics reportedly practiced self-censorship.

On April 26, authorities cancelled a lecture organized by the Najran Cultural Forum by Shia intellectual and author Tawfiq al-Saif, according to the Jeddah-based NGO Adala Center for Human Rights. Authorities gave no reason for the cancellation.

On May 7, local authorities closed Bridges Cafe & Library, a bookstore in Jeddah opened in 2010, amid controversy over liberal speakers lecturing at the venue. Ostensibly, authorities closed the bookstore for carrying banned books, holding events without proper licenses, employing workers illegally, promoting gender-mixing, and remaining open for business during daily prayers.

b. Freedom of Peaceful Assembly and Association

The law does not provide for freedom of assembly and association, which the government strictly limited in practice.

Freedom of Assembly

The law requires a government permit for an organized public assembly of any type, and it was a crime to participate in political protests or unauthorized public assemblies. Security forces reportedly arrested demonstrators and detained them for brief periods.

However, as in 2011, security forces allowed more frequent, small, unauthorized demonstrations throughout the country, despite a March 2011 MOI statement that demonstrations were banned and that it would take "all necessary measures" against those seeking to "disrupt order." In March 2011 the Council of Senior Religious Scholars reinforced the government's stance, stating "demonstrations are prohibited in this country" and explaining that "the correct way in Sharia of realizing common interests is by advising."

Throughout the year authorities continued to allow regular demonstrations in the Eastern Province city of Qatif; however, there were some violent clashes between demonstrators and security forces, and at least six civilians and one policeman were killed (see section 1.a.). Activists reported that security forces used intimidation to discourage people from joining demonstrations. There were also reports of security forces firing bullets in the air to disperse crowds. Videos posted on YouTube purported to portray residents, largely Shia, protesting alleged systematic discrimination and neglect in public investment while showing antiregime slogans written on walls.

On March 8, media reported a woman, Hajer al-Yazidi, died and 50 others were injured when security forces and religious police attempted to disperse a student protest at the women's campus of King Khalid University in Abha. The female student, who suffered from a chronic neurological disorder, died from complications after reportedly receiving a blow to the head.

On July 29, al-Jazeera reported that security forces "opened fire" on protesters and arrested several rioters who were burning tires in Qatif. According to the report, antiriot police injured several individuals by firing live rounds. One individual, reportedly on a "wanted list," was taken to a military hospital with bullet wounds to his back and neck. The government reported there were no casualties.

Freedom of Association

The law does not provide for freedom of association, and the government strictly limited this right in practice. The government prohibited the establishment of political parties or any group it considered as opposing or challenging the regime.

All associations must be licensed by the Ministry of Social Affairs and comply with its regulations. Some groups that advocated for changing elements of the social or political order reported that their licensing requests went unanswered for years despite repeated inquiries. The ministry reportedly used arbitrary means, such as requiring unreasonable types and quantities of information, effectively denying licenses to associations.

In June the BIP charged political activists Mohammed al-Qahtani and Abdullah al-Hamid, both members of the ACPRA, with publicly criticizing national leaders and accusing the government of human rights violations. Their trial lasted until December 29; at year's end both men were free (although they were banned from leaving the country) and awaited the court's ruling.

In February 2011 officials arrested seven of the nine founders of the Islamic Nation Party (Hizb al-Umma al-Islami) for seeking recognition as a political party. According to a Human Rights Watch citation of the request, they appeared to have been detained solely for trying to create a party whose professed aims included "supporting the peaceful reform movement" (see section 3).

Government-chartered associations observed citizen-only limitations. For example, the Saudi Journalists Association, operating under a government charter, prohibited noncitizen members from voting and from attending the association's general assembly.

c. Freedom of Religion

See the Department of State's *International Religious Freedom Report* at www.state.gov/j/drl/irf/rpt.

d. Freedom of Movement, Internally Displaced Persons, Protection of Refugees, and Stateless Persons

The law does not contain provisions for freedom of internal movement, foreign travel, or emigration and repatriation. The government cooperated with the Office of the UN High Commissioner for Refugees (UNHCR) and other humanitarian organizations in providing protection and assistance to internally displaced persons, refugees, returning refugees, asylum seekers, stateless persons, and other persons of concern.

In-country Movement: The government did not generally restrict the free movement of male citizens within the country or the right of citizens to change residence or workplace, provided they held a national identification card (NIC). The law requires all male citizens 15 years old or older to hold a NIC. In November the MOI announced it would start issuing NICs to all female citizens at 15 years of age, phasing in the requirement over a seven-year period. The guardianship system requires a woman to have the permission of her male guardian (normally a father, husband, son, brother, grandfather, uncle, or other male relative) to move freely in the country (see section 6). The government limited driving licenses to men, which effectively prohibited women from driving motor vehicles. On June 17 (marking the first anniversary of the Women2Drive campaign), activists submitted a petition to the king with approximately 800 signatures calling for an end to the ban on women's driving.

Foreign Travel: There are restrictions on foreign travel, including for women and members of minority groups. No one may leave the country without an exit visa and a passport. Women, minors (men younger than age 21), and other dependents of foreign citizen workers under sponsorship require a male guardian's consent to travel abroad. A noncitizen wife needs permission from her husband to travel unless both partners sign a prenuptial agreement permitting the noncitizen wife to travel without the husband's permission. Government entities and male family members can "blacklist" women and minor children, prohibiting their travel. The male guardian is legally able in custody disputes to prevent even adult children from leaving the country.

In April the MOI began allowing male citizens to use the ministry's Web site to register electronic travel permits to their dependents and sponsored expatriate workers. Previously, travel permits could be requested only from branches of the Passport Directorate, and dependents had to present the permits to passport officers upon exiting the country. As part of the new Internet-based system, authorities will notify all registrants by text message to their cell phone whenever any dependent or sponsored foreign citizen worker exits or enters the country. The notification service, which was an elective service since 2010, became automatic for all enrollees on the MOI Web site in November.

Employers or sponsors controlled the departure of foreign workers and residents from the country; employers/sponsors were responsible for processing residence permits and exit visas on their behalf. Sponsors often held their employees' passports, despite a law specifically prohibiting this practice.

The government continued to impose travel bans as part of criminal sentences. The government on occasion reportedly confiscated passports and revoked the rights of some citizens to travel for political reasons but often did not provide them with notification or opportunity to contest the restriction.

During the year the government banned a number of individuals from foreign travel, including Shia cleric Tawfiq al-Amer (see section 1.e.), human rights lawyer Waleed Abu al-Khair (see section 2.a.), and ACPRA cofounders Mohammad al-Qahtani and Abdullah al-Hamid (see section 2.b.).

Protection of Refugees

Access to Asylum: The law provides that the "state will grant political asylum if public interest so dictates." The country has no law implementing this provision, and the UNHCR managed refugee and asylum matters. The government permitted UNHCR-recognized refugees to stay in the country temporarily pending identification of a durable solution. The government generally did not grant asylum or accept refugees for settlement from third countries. Government policy is not to grant refugee status to persons in the country illegally, including those who have overstayed a pilgrimage visa. The government strongly encouraged persons without residency to leave, and it threatened or imposed deportation. Access to naturalization was difficult for refugees. At year's end there were 588 refugees registered with the UNHCR. During the year 12 individuals applied for asylum. The majority of asylum seekers were Iraqi nationals, with smaller numbers of Syrians and Eritreans.

Employment: Refugees and asylum seekers were unable to work legally.

Access to Basic Services: The government reserves for citizens access to education, health care, public housing, courts and judicial procedures, legal services, and other social services. The UNHCR office in Riyadh provided a subsistence allowance covering basic services to a limited number of vulnerable families based on a needs assessment.

Stateless Persons

The country has a significant number of habitual residents who are legally stateless, but data on the stateless population are incomplete and scarce, and the government would not discuss the matter.

Under the Nationality Law, citizenship is derived from the father, but several scenarios lead to stateless children: (1) a child born to an unmarried mother is not affiliated with the father legally, even if the father has recognized the child, and therefore is stateless; (2) when identification documents are withdrawn from a parent, the child also loses his or her identification and accompanying rights (possible when a naturalized parent denaturalizes voluntarily or loses citizenship through other acts); (3) children of a citizen mother and a noncitizen father are without nationality, unless they acquire citizenship from the father; and (4) children of a citizen father and a noncitizen mother are noncitizens, unless the government has authorized the marriage of the parents prior to birth. Additionally, when government authorities withdraw a citizen's NIC, his or her children also lose their citizenship.

The UNHCR unofficially estimated there were approximately 70,000 stateless persons in the country, almost all of whom were native-born Arab residents known locally as Bidoon (an Arabic word that means "without" [citizenship]); there were also some Baloch, West Africans, and several hundred thousand Rohingya Muslims from Burma; however, only a portion of these communities were stateless. For example, many Rohingya had expired passports that their home governments refused to renew.

Bidoon are persons whose ancestors failed to obtain nationality, such as descendants of nomadic tribes not counted among the native tribes during the reign of the country's founder, King Abdulaziz; descendants of foreign-born fathers who arrived before there were laws regulating citizenship; and rural migrants whose parents failed to register their births. As noncitizens Bidoon are unable to obtain passports or travel abroad. The government denied them employment and educational opportunities, and their marginalized status made them among the poorest residents of the country. In recent years the Ministry of Education encouraged them to attend school. The government issues Bidoon five-year residency permits to facilitate their social integration in government-provided health care and other services, putting them on similar footing with sponsored foreign workers.

There were an estimated 240,000 Palestinians residents, who were not registered as refugees, as the mandate of the UN Refugee and Works Agency to protect and assist Palestinian refugees is limited to the West Bank, Gaza, Lebanon, Syria, and Jordan.

Section 3. Respect for Political Rights: The Right of Citizens to Change Their Government

The law does not provide citizens the right to change their government peacefully and establishes the Al Saud family monarchy as the political system. The law provides citizens the right to communicate with public authorities on any matter, and the government is established on the principle of consultation (shura). The king and senior officials, including ministers and regional governors, are required to make themselves available by holding meetings (majlis), open-door events where in theory any male citizen or noncitizen may express an opinion or a grievance without the need for an appointment. Most government ministries and agencies had women's sections to interact with female citizens and noncitizens, and at least one regional governorate hired female employees to receive women's petitions. Only a few members of the ruling family have a voice in the choice of leaders, the composition of the government, or changes to the political system. The Allegiance Commission, composed of up to 35 senior princes appointed by the king, is responsible for selecting a king and crown prince upon the death or incapacitation of either.

Elections and Political Participation

Recent Elections: In September 2011 following a two-year postponement, the government held elections for the second time since 1963 for the country's 285 municipal councils; elected candidates filled half of the 1,632 seats, while the king appointed the other half. As in the first elections in 2005, participation was limited to civilian male citizens at least 21 years old. Uniformed members of the security forces, including the military and police, were ineligible to vote. According to the Municipal Council Elections Committee, there was no legal prohibition against women voting; however, as was the case in 2005, the committee cited logistical and other technical reasons why women were not allowed to vote or run for office. More than 1,700 lawyers from the National Committee of Lawyers monitored the elections nationally, and the organization assessed that the elections were fair and transparent. The NSHR, however, refused to observe the elections, protesting women's ineligibility to vote or seek election. Candidates were not permitted to contest under party affiliation. Following the elections, the king issued a royal decree permitting women to vote and run in future municipal council elections.

Political Parties: There were no political parties or similar associations. In February 2011, one week after a group of nine individuals submitted a request for recognition of the Islamic Nation Party (Hizb al-Umma al-Islami) as a political party to the Royal Court and the Consultative Council, authorities arrested seven of the party's nine founders. According to the party's Web site, authorities demanded that the founders sign a legally binding promise to withdraw their names from the party's founding document. All members of the group that signed such a statement were released. Abdulaziz al-Wuhaibi refused to do so and was sentenced to seven years in prison. In November the appeals court for the Specialized Criminal Court overturned his sentence as too lenient and ordered a retrial. In December the authorities ordered al-Wuhaibi to undergo a psychological evaluation to determine whether he was responsible for the commission of any crime. He remained in detention at year's end.

Participation of Women and Minorities: Discrimination based on widespread gender segregation excluded women from many aspects of public life, including from formal decision-making positions. However, women increasingly participated in political life, albeit with significantly less status than men did. There were 12 female advisers to the 150-person royally appointed Consultative Council, which advises the king and can propose legislation. In September 2011 the king issued a royal decree providing for the appointment of women to serve as full Consultative Council members at the beginning of the term in 2013. There were no women on the High Court (women's ability to practice law is severely limited) or Supreme Judicial Council. There are no women judges or prosecutors.

On October 8, local media reported that the Ministry of Justice had started accepting applications from women to be licensed as lawyers. On December 16, a royal decree was issued to expedite the process of opening separate offices in courts to be staffed by women. There were two women in senior-level government positions, as deputy minister for women's education and deputy minister for women's higher education, in addition to senior advisors in multiple ministries. The country had a number of female diplomats. Women working in the security services were largely restricted to employment in female prisons, at women's universities, and in clerical positions in police stations where they were responsible for visually identifying other women for law enforcement purposes.

There are no laws that prevent male minorities from participating in political life on the same basis as other male citizens, but societal discrimination marginalized the Shia population. While the religious affiliation of Consultative Council members was not publicly known, the council included an estimated five or six Shia members. There were no known religious minorities in the cabinet. Multiple municipal Councils in the Eastern Province, where most Saudi Shia are concentrated, had large proportions of Shia as members to reflect the local population, including a majority in Qatif and 50 percent in al-Hasa. At year's end there were some Eastern Province Shia judges dealing with intra-Shia personal status and family laws.

Section 4. Corruption and Lack of Transparency in Government

The law provides criminal penalties for official corruption; however, the government did not implement the law effectively, and officials engaged in corrupt practices with impunity. There were reports of government corruption during the year, including a perception of corruption by some members of the royal family and the executive branch of the government.

In November a senior official from the Jeddah municipality was convicted of corruption and negligence, fined one million riyals ($267,000), and sentenced to seven years in prison; two businessmen also were convicted of bribery and also fined and imprisoned. The verdict was part of ongoing investigations and trials of municipal officials and others accused of corruption because of 2009 and 2011 Jeddah floods.

Public officials were not subject to financial disclosure laws.

Government employees who accept bribes face 10 years in prison or fines up to one million riyals ($267,000). The National Anti-Corruption Commission, established by the king in March 2011, was responsible for promoting transparency and combating all forms of financial and administrative corruption; the commission's ministerial-level director reported directly to the king. In September the National Anti-Corruption Commission reported that it received approximately 100 reports per day; the commission investigated these reports and then forwarded relevant cases and its findings to the CIB and the BIP for appropriate action. During the year the commission actively campaigned against corruption and had a hotline for reporting such abuses. However, the CIB remains responsible for investigating financial malfeasance, and the BIP has the lead on all criminal investigations.

The law does not provide for, and there is no right to, public access to government information, such as ministerial budgets or allocations to members of the royal family.

Section 5. Governmental Attitude Regarding International and Nongovernmental Investigation of Alleged Violations of Human Rights

The law provides that "the State shall protect human rights in accordance with the Islamic Sharia"; however, the government restricted the activities of, while at times cooperating to varying degrees with, domestic and international human rights organizations in investigations of alleged violations of human rights. The HRC stated that the government welcomed the visits of legitimate, unbiased human rights groups but added that the government could not act on the "hundreds of requests," in part because it was cumbersome to decide which domestic agency would be their interlocutor.

The government often cooperated with and sometimes accepted the recommendations of the NSHR, the sole government-licensed domestic human rights organization. The NSHR accepted requests for assistance and complaints about government actions affecting human rights.

The government viewed two active but unlicensed human rights groups, the Human Rights First Society (HRFS) and the ACPRA, with suspicion and claimed they meddled in government affairs. At year's end the government had not licensed the HRFS, whose founder, Ibrahim al-Mugaiteeb, applied for a license in 2002. The government continued to permit its informal operation, but since the group was formally "unlicensed," it remained unclear which activities the group could undertake without risking punishment, and even "permitted" activities could be criticized by the government. Without a license, the group was unable to raise operating funds, which severely limited its activities. ACPRA applied for a license in 2008, which was not granted; however, the government allowed its unlicensed operation. Authorities blocked both HRFS and ACPRA's Web sites during the year.

An abortive attempt to create a political organization, accompanied by a petition calling for political reform, preceded the 2007 arrests of nine men who, along with seven others, were held without formal charges until August 2010. In November 2011 a court in Riyadh convicted a group of 16 men, led by former judge Suliman al-Reshoudi, on a range of charges that included allegedly forming a secret organization, attempting to seize power, inciting discontent against the king, financing terrorism, and money laundering. The men received sentences that varied from 10 to 30 years and included travel bans and fines; a number of them planned to appeal their sentences, but there had been no development as of year's end.

Government Human Rights Bodies: The HRC is part of the government. The HRC president has ministerial status and reports to the king. According to the NSHR's 2009 report, the HRC "met with weak collaboration on the part of some governmental bodies in spite of the issuance of royal directives." The adequately resourced HRC was effective in highlighting problems and registering and responding to complaints received, but its capacity to effect change was more limited. The HRC worked directly with the Royal Diwan and the Council of Ministers; with a committee composed of representatives of the Consultative Council and the Ministries of Labor, Social Affairs, and Interior; and with Consultative Council Committees for the Judiciary, Islamic Affairs, and Human Rights. During the year HRC and NSHR were more outspoken in areas deemed less politically sensitive, including child abuse, child marriage, and prison conditions. They avoided topics such as protests and indefinite detentions that would otherwise require directly confronting government authorities. The HRC Board's membership included at least two Shia out of 19 full-time members, who received and responded to complaints submitted to them by their constituencies, including issues related to religious freedom and women's rights.

Section 6. Discrimination, Societal Abuses, and Trafficking in Persons

The law prohibits discrimination based on race but not gender, disability, language, sexual orientation and gender identity, or social status. The law and tradition discriminated based on gender. The law and the guardianship system restrict women to the status of a legal dependent vis-a-vis their male guardians. This status is unchanged even after women reach adulthood. Women and some men faced widespread and state-enforced segregation based on societal, cultural, and religious traditions.

The government generally reinforced Sharia-based traditional prohibitions on discrimination based on disability, language, social status, or race.

Women

Rape and Domestic Violence: Rape is a criminal offense under Sharia with a wide range of penalties from flogging to execution. The government enforced the law based on its interpretation of Sharia, and courts punished victims for illegal "mixing of genders," as well as the perpetrator even when there was no conviction for rape. Consequently, due to the legal and social penalties, few cases were brought to trial. The government did not recognize spousal rape. Statistics on incidents of rape were not available, but press reports and observers indicated rape was a serious problem. The government did not maintain public records on prosecutions, convictions, or punishments. Most rape cases were unreported because victims faced societal reprisal, diminished marriage opportunities, criminal sanction up to imprisonment, or accusations of adultery.

There were no laws criminalizing violence specifically against women, and the law does not distinguish domestic violence within the general legal prohibition against violence. Researchers stated that domestic violence may be seriously underreported, making it difficult to gauge the magnitude of the problem, which they believed to be widespread. Independent estimates supported by officials working at the Ministry of Social Affairs indicated that the incidence of female spousal abuse ranged widely, from 16 to 50 percent of all wives. Officials stated that the government did not clearly define domestic violence and that procedures concerning cases, and accordingly enforcement, varied from one government body to another. NSHR's 2011 annual report noted that the organization investigated 370 cases of domestic violence and violations of women's rights compared with 282 such cases in 2010. Noting that family violence was an increasing problem, the Ministry of Social Affairs reported that the number of family violence incidents against women in 2011 reached 931 cases. Violence included a broad spectrum of abuse. There were reports of police or judges returning women directly to their abusers, most of whom were the women's legal guardians. The government made efforts to combat domestic violence, and the King Abdulaziz Center for National Dialogue held workshops and distributed educational materials on peaceful conflict resolution between spouses and in families.

The government supported family protection shelters. During the year the HRC received complaints of domestic abuse and referred these complaints to other government offices. During 2011 the HRC's women and children's branches throughout the kingdom received 350 complaints including 71 from women; domestic violence and abuse accounted for most cases. The HRC advised complainants and offered legal assistance to some female litigants. The organization provided facilities for children of women complainants and litigants, and it distributed publications supporting women's rights in education, health care, development, and the workplace.

Sexual Harassment: The extent of sexual harassment was difficult to measure with little media reporting and no government data. The government's interpretation of Sharia guides courts on cases of sexual harassment. Employers in many sectors maintained separate male and female workspaces where feasible.

Reproductive Rights: There were no reports of government interference in a couple's right to decide freely and responsibly the number, spacing, and timing of children and to have the information and means to do so free from discrimination, coercion, and violence. Prenatal and postpartum care was available, but patients were not always aware of its availability, and medical staff did not always emphasize its importance. Intrauterine devices were the most popular form of birth control, and women, regardless of marital status, were legally able to obtain them. Birth control pills also were available to women in local pharmacies without prescriptions. Although no legal barriers prevented access to contraception, in practice many women were limited by constraints on mobility and economic resources as well as social pressure for large families. Information was not available regarding equal diagnosis and treatment of sexually transmitted infections.

Discrimination: Women continued to face significant discrimination under law and custom, and many remained uninformed about their unequal rights. Although they may legally own property and are entitled to financial support from their guardian, women have fewer political or social rights than men, and society treats them as unequal members in the political and social spheres. The country's interpretation of Sharia prohibits women from marrying non-Muslims, but men may marry Christians and Jews. Women require government permission to marry noncitizens; men must obtain government permission if they intend to marry noncitizens from countries other than Gulf Cooperation Council member states Bahrain, Kuwait, Oman, Qatar, and the United Arab Emirates. Women do not directly transmit citizenship to their children.

The guardianship system requires that every woman have a close male relative as her "guardian" with the legal authority to approve her travel outside of the country (see section 2.d.). A guardian also has authority to approve some types of business licenses and study at a university or college. Women can make their own determinations concerning hospital care. Women can work without their guardian's permission; however, most employers required women have their guardian's permission. A husband who "verbally" (rather than via a court process) divorces his wife or refuses to sign final divorce papers continues to be her legal guardian.

Widespread societal exclusion enforced by but not limited to state institutions restricted women from using many public facilities. Women usually are required to sit in separate, specially designated family sections. They frequently are not allowed to consume food in restaurants that do not have such sections. Women risk arrest for riding in a private vehicle driven by a male who is not an employee or a close male relative. Cultural norms enforced by state institutions require women to wear an abaya (a loose-fitting, full-length black cloak) in public. The religious police also generally expected Muslim women to cover their hair and non-Muslim women from Asian and African countries to comply more fully with local customs of dress than non-Muslim Western women. In some rural areas and smaller cities, women adhered to the traditional dress code covering the entire body, including hands, feet, hair, and face.

Women also faced discrimination in courts, where the testimony of one man equals that of two women. All judges are male, and women faced restriction on their practice of law. In divorce proceedings women must demonstrate legally specified grounds for divorce, but men can divorce without giving cause. In doing so men are required to pay immediately an amount of money agreed at the time of the marriage that serves as a one-time alimony payment; however, men can be forced to make subsequent alimony payments by court order. Women who demonstrate legal grounds for divorce are entitled to alimony.

Women faced discrimination under family law. For example, a woman needs a guardian's permission to marry or must seek a court order in the case of adhl (male guardians refusing marriage of women under their charge). In such adhl cases, the judge assumes the role of the guardian and can approve the marriage. Courts award custody of children when they attain a specified age (seven years for boys and nine years for girls) to the divorced husband or the deceased husband's family. In numerous cases former husbands prevented divorced noncitizen women from visiting their children. Women are also discriminated against under inheritance laws, where daughters receive half the inheritance awarded to their brothers.

According to recent surveys, women constituted more than 58 percent of university students; education through university level was generally segregated. The only exceptions to segregation in higher education were medical schools at the undergraduate level and the King Abdullah University of Science and Technology, a graduate-level research university, where women worked jointly with men, were not required to wear the veil, and drove cars on campus.

The Ministry of Labor explicitly approves and encourages the employment of women in specific sectors.

In July 2011 the Ministry of Labor issued regulations requiring all stores selling women's undergarments and cosmetics to be staffed solely by women. In

November the ministry announced implementation of this regulation. The 2011 regulations also ban women from 20 professions, mostly in heavy industry, but creates guidelines for women to telework. In November the Board of Grievances began recruiting women to work in its judicial offices across the country answering inquiries, registering cases, delivering copies of verdicts, and checking the identity of female clients. A 2010 report by the central bank estimated that 36,000 female citizens worked in the public sector and 48,000 in the private sector, in a total labor force of more than nine million. The vast majority of the 1.4 million women working in the kingdom were foreign laborers with significant additional restrictions on their rights. There were cases during the year of women workers fleeing their sponsors because of reported abuse (see section 7).

Widespread gender segregation directly led to discrimination in employment. Despite gender segregation the law grants women the right to obtain business licenses with the approval of their guardians, and women frequently obtained licenses in fields that might require them to supervise foreign workers, interact with male clients, or deal with government officials. In medical settings and in the energy industry, women and men worked together, and in some instances women supervised male employees. Women who work in establishments with 50 or more female employees have the right to maternity leave and childcare.

Children

Birth Registration: Citizenship derives from the father, and only the father can register a birth. There were cases of children of citizen parents being denied public services, including education and health care, because the government failed to register the birth entirely or immediately.

Child Abuse: Abuse of children occurred, but information was sparse. In 2011 the NSHR registered 95 instances of violence against children, according to its annual report.

Child Marriage: There were reports during the year of child marriage, although it was almost entirely limited to rural areas. Senior government officials spoke out against the practice and advocated the adoption of a minimum marriage age. Sharia does not specify a minimum age for marriage but suggests girls may marry after reaching puberty. According to some senior religious leaders, girls as young as age 10 may be married. Families sometimes arranged such marriages, principally in rural areas or to settle family debts, without the consent of the child. The HRC and NSHR monitored cases of child marriages, which they reported were rare or, at least, rarely reported. The bride's age must be recorded in the application for a marriage license, and registration of the marriage is a legal prerequisite for consummation. The government reportedly instructed marriage registrars not to register marriages involving children.

Sexual Exploitation of Children: The Anti-Cyber Crimes Law stipulates that imprisonment and fines for crimes including the preparation, publication, and promotion of material for pornographic sites may be no less than two and one-half years' imprisonment or 1.5 million riyals ($400,000) if the crime includes the exploitation of minors. The law does not define a minimum age for consensual sex.

International Child Abduction: The kingdom is not a party to the 1980 Hague Convention on the Civil Aspects of International Child Abduction. For country-specific information
see http://travel.state.gov/abduction/country/country_3781.html.

Anti-Semitism

There were no known Jewish citizens and no statistics available concerning the religious denominations of foreigners.

According to the Ministry of Islamic Affairs, no imams publicly espoused intolerant views warranting dismissal during the year. In contrast with previous years, there were no reports that Sunni imams, who receive government stipends, used anti-Jewish, anti-Christian, and anti-Shia language in their sermons. During the year the ministry issued periodic circulars to clerics and imams in mosques directing them to include messages on the principles of justice, equality, and tolerance and to encourage rejection of bigotry and all forms of racial discrimination in their sermons.

The government's multiyear project to revise textbooks, curricula, and teaching methods to promote tolerance and remove content disparaging religions other than Islam began in 2007. At year's end new curricula and textbooks had been developed for grades four through nine; however, despite these efforts some intolerant material remained in textbooks used in schools.

Editorial cartoons occasionally exhibited anti-Semitism characterized by stereotypical images of Jews along with Jewish symbols, particularly at times of heightened political tension with Israel. Anti-Semitic comments by journalists, academics, and clerics occasionally appeared in the media. On August 13, Salman al-Awdah, a popular cleric who holds no official position, stated during an interview on a private satellite television channel that while the Holocaust has "an historical basis," it has become "exaggerated" and a "source for extortion." Al-Awdah continued that "the role of the Jews is to wreak destruction, wage war, and to practice deception and extortion." He then told a story claiming that Jews use human blood to make Passover matzos.

Trafficking in Persons

See the Department of State's *Trafficking in Persons Report* at www.state.gov/j/tip.

Persons with Disabilities

The law does not prohibit discrimination against persons with physical, sensory, intellectual, and mental disabilities in employment, education, air travel and other transportation, access to health care, or the provision of other state services or other areas. There is no legislation mandating public accessibility to buildings, information, and communications. Newer commercial buildings often included such access, as did some newer government buildings. Children with disabilities could attend government-supported schools. Persons with disabilities had equal access to information and communications.

Information about patterns of abuse of persons with disabilities in prisons and educational and mental health institutions was not available. The Ministry of Social Affairs is responsible for protecting the rights of persons with disabilities. Vocational rehabilitation projects and social care programs increasingly brought persons with disabilities into the mainstream.

National/Racial/Ethnic Minorities

Although racial discrimination is illegal, societal discrimination against members of national, racial, ethnic, or tribal minorities was a problem. Foreign workers from Africa and Asia were subjected to formal and informal discrimination, especially racial discrimination. The tolerance campaign of the King Abdulaziz Center for National Dialogue sought to address some of these problems.

There were numerous cases of assault against foreign workers and reports of widespread worker abuse. The Shia minority continued to suffer social, legal, economic, and political discrimination. To address the problem, the Ministries of Defense and Interior and the National Guard held antidiscrimination training courses in recent years for police and law enforcement officers. In contrast to previous years, there were no reports of training during the year or of the success rate of these programs.

Societal Abuses, Discrimination, and Acts of Violence Based on Sexual Orientation and Gender Identity

Under Sharia as interpreted in the country, consensual same-sex sexual conduct is punishable by death or flogging. It is illegal for men "to behave like women" or to wear women's clothes and vice versa. Due to social conventions and potential persecution, lesbian, gay, bisexual, and transgender organizations did not operate openly, nor were there gay rights advocacy events of any kind. There were reports of official societal discrimination, physical violence, and harassment based on sexual orientation or gender identity in employment, housing, statelessness, access to education, and health care. Stigma or intimidation likely limited reports of incidents of abuse. Sexual orientation and gender identity could constitute the basis for harassment, blackmail, or other actions.

On April 17, authorities announced "gays, tomboys, and emos [counterculture youth]" would not be allowed to enter public schools and universities until they changed their "appearance and behavior." The CPVPV announced receiving high-level orders to enforce these new rules on homosexuality on "girls who adopt masculine appearances" and those emulating the "emo" subculture.

On December 18, a court sentenced an unnamed head of a government office in Baha to 25 years in jail and 2,000 lashings in public. Authorities charged the individuals with staging "unethical parties," taking drugs, extorting other officials, and "involvement in sodomy." Media also reported the official was fined 200,000 riyals ($53,330) and banned from travelling outside the country. The official's aide was sentenced to 15 years in jail and 1,500 public lashings in addition to a travel ban. The judge also reportedly issued a recommendation that the two not benefit from any future pardon.

There were no government efforts to address potential discrimination.

Other Societal Violence or Discrimination

There was no reported societal violence or discrimination against persons with HIV/AIDS. By law the government deported foreign workers who tested positive for HIV/AIDS upon arrival or when hospitalized for other reasons. There was no indication that HIV-positive foreigners failed to receive antiretroviral treatment or that authorities isolated them during the year. The Ministry of Health's HIV/AIDS program worked to fight stigma and discrimination against persons with HIV/AIDS.

Section 7. Worker Rights

a. Freedom of Association and the Right to Collective Bargaining

The law does not provide for the right of workers to form and join independent unions. The law does not protect the right to collective bargaining or the right to conduct legal strikes. The law does not protect against antiunion discrimination or require reinstatement of workers fired for union activity.

There are no labor unions in the country, and workers face potential dismissal, imprisonment, or, in the case of migrant workers, deportation for union activities. The Commission for the Settlement of Labor Disputes under the Ministry of Labor investigates labor-related complaints by private individuals against officials responsible for the enforcement of the provisions of the kingdom's labor laws.

The government allows citizen-only labor committees in workplaces with more than 100 employees, but the government places undue limitations on the right of association and is heavily involved in the formation and activities of these committees. For example, the Ministry of Labor approves the committee members and authorizes ministry and employer representatives who can attend committee meetings. The minutes of the meetings must be submitted to management and then transmitted to the minister; the ministry can dissolve committees if they violate regulations or are deemed to threaten public security. Committees are limited to making recommendations to company management regarding only improvements to work conditions, health and safety, productivity, and training programs.

Freedom of association and the right to collective bargaining were not respected in practice.

b. Prohibition of Forced or Compulsory Labor

The law prohibits forced or compulsory labor; however, the government did not effectively enforce legal protections for migrant workers, and the labor law does not apply to domestic employees, the largest group of workers susceptible to forced labor conditions.

Forced labor occurred, especially among migrant workers, domestic servants, and children. Conditions indicative of forced labor experienced by foreign workers included withholding of passports, nonpayment of wages, restrictions on movement, and verbal, physical, and sexual abuse. Many noncitizen workers, particularly domestic employees, were not able to exercise their right to end their contractual work. Restrictive sponsorship laws increased workers' vulnerability to forced labor conditions and made many foreign workers reluctant to report abuse. An estimated five million foreigners resided illegally in the country, most of whom were believed to have come as pilgrims and overstayed their visas. As of a result of their illegal status, these individuals were susceptible to forced labor.

Also see the Department of State's *Trafficking in Persons Report* at www.state.gov/j/tip.

c. Prohibition of Child Labor and Minimum Age for Employment

The law states no person younger than 15 years old may legally work unless that person is the sole source of support for the family. Children between 13 and 15 years old may work if the job is not harmful to health or growth and does not interfere with schooling. The law states that legal minors may not be employed in hazardous operations or harmful industries; children under 18 may not be employed for shifts exceeding six hours a day. There is no minimum age for workers employed in family-owned businesses or other areas considered extensions of the household, such as farming, herding, and domestic service.

The HRC and the NSHR are responsible for enforcing the country's child labor laws. However, there was little information on government efforts to enforce relevant laws or actions to prevent or eliminate child labor during the year. The most common enforcement was to complaints of children begging on the streets.

Child labor occurred in practice, most commonly in the form of children, usually from other countries including Yemen and Ethiopia, being forced into child begging rings, street vending, and work in family businesses. Although in previous years there were reports of foreign domestic workers younger than 18 (some of whom reportedly traveled to the country with forged documents), such abuses could not be confirmed during the year.

d. Acceptable Conditions of Work

The monthly minimum wage for public sector employees was 3,000 riyals ($800). There was no private sector minimum wage for foreign workers; however, the government's Nitaqaat (Saudization) program set a general minimum wage for citizens at 3,000 riyals per month. The law does not provide for equal pay for equal work.

The Commission for the Settlement of Labor Disputes actively prosecuted cases against employers of citizens, with most cases favoring the employee. Prosecution of employers of noncitizens occurred with less frequency, and most verdicts reportedly favored the employer. Labor regulations ostensibly apply to all workers in the public and private sector other than domestic servants, provide for a 48-hour standard workweek at regular pay, a weekly 24-hour rest period (normally on Fridays, although the employer may grant it on another day), and time-and-a-half pay for overtime, with a maximum of 12 additional hours per week. However, the law's provisions were not enforced.

In April the Ministry of Labor announced the creation of 1,000 additional labor inspector positions to investigate labor law violations; however, it was unclear how many of these individuals had been hired by year's end. The law penalizes individuals between 500 riyals ($133) and 1,000 riyals ($267) for bringing foreigners into the country to work in any service, including domestic service, without following the required procedures and obtaining a permit.

The labor law provides for regular safety inspections and enables Ministry of Labor-appointed inspectors to examine materials used or handled in industrial and other operations and to submit samples of suspected hazardous materials or substances to government laboratories. The Ministry of Health's Occupational Health Service Directorate works with the Labor Ministry on health and safety matters. Regulations require employers to protect some workers from job-related hazards and disease, although some violations occurred. These regulations did not cover farmers, herdsmen, domestic servants, or workers in family-operated businesses. Foreign nationals privately reported frequent failures to enforce health and safety standards.

Labor regulations provide for a maximum of 12 additional hours of overtime per week. This regulation does not distinguish between different types of employment.

The law requires foreign workers be sponsored by a citizen or business to obtain legal work and residency status. The law does not permit some noncitizens to change their workplace without their sponsor's permission. This forces these workers to remain with the sponsor until fulfillment of the contract or seek the assistance of their embassy to return home. Sponsors with commercial or labor disputes with foreign employees could also ask authorities to prohibit the employees from departing the country until the dispute was resolved. However, under Nitaqaat the sponsorship of foreign workers working at companies not meeting specific goals for employing citizens as a percent of their workforce lapses, and these workers may transfer their sponsorship to a new firm without having to leave the country, seek permission from their original sponsor, or apply for a new visa.

The Ministry of Labor's Migrant Workers' Welfare Department is responsible for addressing cases of abuse and exploitation among migrant workers. Noncitizen workers were able to submit complaints and seek help from the 37 offices throughout the country, although the government was generally unresponsive. The Ministry of Labor reportedly maintained a database of abusive employers and occasionally banned individuals and companies who mistreated noncitizen workers from sponsoring such workers for up to five years; however, the ministry did not provide any examples of employers banned during the year.

Bilateral labor agreements set conditions on foreign workers' minimum wage; housing; benefits including leave, medical care; and other topics. These provisions were not necessarily drafted with reference to international standards, and they varied depending on the sending country's relative bargaining leverage. The Labor Law and the Anti-Trafficking Law provide penalties for abuse of such workers.

During 2011 both Indonesia and the Philippines banned new domestic workers from working in the country while they sought improved contract terms for their citizens. The Philippines also requested that prospective employers provide bank statements. At year's end the Indonesian ban remained in place. However, in October the Saudi and Philippine governments concluded a bilateral work agreement, and Philippine officials lifted the ban, allowing Philippine domestic workers to deploy to the kingdom for the first time since June 2011. As part of the agreement, the government agreed to enforce a minimum wage of 1,500 riyals

($400 per month) and again committed to prevent contract substitution and the seizure of workers' passports.

In August 2011 the Ministry of Labor mandated the establishment of fewer and larger expatriate labor recruitment firms, ostensibly better to protect migrant workers, including domestic workers. At the end of the year, 13 unified recruitment firms were registered.

The government engaged in a news campaign highlighting the plight of abused workers, trained law enforcement and other officials on combating trafficking in persons, and worked with the embassies of labor-sending countries to disseminate information about labor rights to foreign workers. During Ramadan the HRC broadcast a public awareness program on television emphasizing the Islamic injunction to treat employees well.

An estimated 8.4 million noncitizen workers, including approximately 1.5 million female domestic employees, made up the majority of the country's labor force. There were also an estimated five million illegal residents in the country, most of whom were thought to be workers. Legal workers generally negotiated and agreed to conditions prior to arrival in the country, in accordance with the contract requirements contained in the labor law; nevertheless, many found themselves subjected to different conditions, such as delays in payment of wages, changes in employer, or changed working hours and conditions. Migrant workers, especially domestic workers, were vulnerable to abuse, exploitation, and conditions contravening labor laws, including nonpayment of wages, working for periods in excess of the 48-hour week, working for periods longer than the prescribed eight-hour workday, and restrictions on movement due to passport confiscation. There were also reports of physical and verbal abuse.

On November 25, a Saudi man was arrested after he clubbed his maid to death in his home in Jeddah. At year's end there was no further information on the case.

According to a June 2011 *Arab News* article, local authorities in the southern province of Jizan discovered a 45-year-old Sri Lankan maid, Indrani Mallika Hettiarachchi, who had been kept against her will without pay for nearly 14 years by her employer; authorities subsequently arrested the employer. There was no further information during the year.

Many noncitizen workers, particularly domestic employees, were not able to exercise their right to remove themselves from dangerous situations. Some employers physically prevented workers from leaving or threatened them with nonpayment of wages if they left. Sponsoring employers, who controlled foreign workers' ability to remain employed and in the country, usually held foreign workers' passports, a practice prohibited by law. In some contract disputes, a sponsor held the employee in country until the dispute was resolved to force the employee to accept a disadvantageous settlement or risk deportation without any settlement.

Foreign workers could contact the labor offices of their embassies for assistance. During the year hundreds of domestic workers sought shelter at their embassies, some fleeing sexual abuse or other violence. Some embassies maintained safe houses for citizens fleeing situations that amounted to bondage. The workers usually sought legal help from embassies and government agencies to obtain end of service benefits and exit visas.

In addition to their embassies, domestic employees may contact the NSHR; the HRC; the governmental Permanent Committee to Combat Human Trafficking; and the Ministry of Labor's Migrant Workers' Welfare Department, which provided services to safeguard migrant workers' rights and to protect them from abuse. Workers may also apply to the offices of regional governors and may lodge an appeal with the Board of Grievances against decisions from those authorities.